Best Editorial Cartoons of the Year

BEST EDITORIAL CARTOONS OF THE YEAR

1980 EDITION

Edited by
CHARLES BROOKS

Foreword by
DANIEL PATRICK MOYNIHAN

PELICAN PUBLISHING COMPANY
GRETNA 1980

Special acknowledgments are made to the following for permission to use copyrighted material in this volume:

Editorial cartoons by Timothy Atseff, © Richmond Syndicate; Dick Locher, © Chicago Tribune—New York News Syndicate; Al Liederman, © Rothco; Art Henrikson, © Paddock Publications; Paul Fell, © Maverick Media, Inc.; Jeff MacNelly, © Chicago Tribune—New York News Syndicate; Herc Ficklen, © Avalon Features; Ben Wicks, © Toronto Sun Syndicate; Art Poinier, © United Features Syndicate; Ed Valtman, © Rothco; Ed Stein, © NEA; Jimmy Margulies, © Rothco; John Milt Morris, © The Associated Press; Jim Berry, © NEA; Dave Granlund, © NEA; Eldon Pletcher, © Rothco; Doug Sneyd, © Sneyd Syndicate; Jerry Robinson, © Cartoonists and Writers Syndicate; Steve Greenberg, © Van Nuys Publishing Co.; Jack Bender, © Rothco; Mike Konopacki, © Rothco; Frank Interlandi, © Los Angeles Times Syndicate; Mark Taylor, © Rothco; Draper Hill, © The Detroit News, distributed by King Features Syndicate; Hugh Haynie, © Los Angeles Times Syndicate; and Dick Wallmeyer, © Register and Tribune Syndicate.

Library of Congress Serial Catalog Data

Best editorial cartoons. 1972-
    Gretna [La.] Pelican Pub. Co.
    v. 29cm. annual-
"A pictorial history of the year."

    I. United States—Politics and government—
1969—Caricatures and Cartoons—Periodicals.
E839.5.B45   320.9'7309240207   73-643645
ISSN 0091-2220   MARC-S

Manufactured in the United States of America
Published by Pelican Publishing Company, Inc.
1101 Monroe Street, Gretna, Louisiana 70053
Designed by Barney McKee

Contents

Open Letter to a Soviet Citizen

The Soviet Union last year banned this annual series, the *Best Editorial Cartoons of the Year*, from the Moscow International Book Fair. The reason? The ideas expressed are too dangerous to Marxist ideology.

It has been sixty-two years since Russia's "glorious" October Revolution elevated Marxism to a governmental power base. What a weak, pitiful ideology it must be, and what shallow roots it must have, if the light of truth still poses such a threat after more than half a century. There are those who still proclaim that Marxism is the wave of the future. It is not. It is the wave of the past. Indeed, it is the worst of the past. Remarkably primitive in its evolution, it is an anachronism in modern society.

In the development of rights even for its own elite few, Marxism has not yet reached the year 1215, when noblemen wrested the Magna Carta from King John of England. In the development of the right to publish and read, it has not yet reached the year 1644 when my illustrious forebear, John Milton, penned *Areopagitica*, that marvelous, studied argument in behalf of freedom of the press. Not even the divine right of kings nor the authority of commissars can be permitted to censor in a mature society.

In the development of the right of men to govern themselves, Soviet Marxism has not reached the year 930 when the Icelandic parliament was created, nor 1689, when the rights of ordinary citizens in England were guaranteed.

In the development of religious freedom, it has not yet reached the year 1792, when the Baptists of Virginia demanded, and won, passage of the First Amendment to the United States Constitution which freed them from religious persecution. But citizens such as Georgi Vins, the Ukrainian Baptist, nevertheless are still imprisoned or deported when they attempt to exercise that right.

In economic development, your country remains pre-agricultural, harking back to the misty beginnings of civilization when man was barely able to feed himself. Marxist policy has never produced enough food for its populace—and I daresay it never will. In spite of Marxism's record of producing less and less for fewer and fewer people, some self-styled intellectuals, political leaders, and college professors here in the United States have become enamored with it. Endless hours are spent discussing its bankrupt theories, and college students are required to complete lengthy assignments on the subject.

Some of this fascination is due to ignorance, of course, but one driving force has been the desire of the few to direct and to control the lives of the many. That desire, unfortunately, is a basic human trait, veiled only thinly by civilization. This concept of controlling people's lives stands as the crowning achievement of Marxism and Russian national socialism. Marxism, in fact, has been more ruthlessly efficient in killing and repressing its population than any other political system devised by man. The other system of national socialism, in Nazi Germany, killed six million men, women, and children, while the national socialist government of the Soviet Union caused the deaths of twenty-five million farmers in Russia's early history alone.

Here I offer my mea culpa. The people of the United States—myself included—who prize freedom have not vigorously enough demanded a higher commitment to human freedom throughout the world. We have allowed our politicians, so-called intellectuals, and influence-makers to ignore Marxist assaults against human rights while flailing away at the pygmies who inefficiently place limits on human rights.

May I offer an example? In 1976 the Association of American Publishers invited the chairman of the Committee on Human Rights of the U.S. House of Representatives, Donald Fraser, to address the membership on the subject of human rights. This, you may recall, was three years after Alexander Solzhenitsyn had stunned the world with the revelations in his *Gulag Archipelago*. Summing up his speech, Congressman Fraser declared that if human rights problems could be solved in Greece, South Korea, South Africa, and Chile, human rights would then be extended throughout the world. He studiously avoided any mention of the Soviet Union.

Challenged after the speech as to why he had not even mentioned rights violations in the Soviet Union, Fraser snapped: "We can't do anything about them!" The editor-in-chief of a major educational publishing house, standing nearby, leaped to his support.

Such cynicism. Such callousness. What better example could anyone find of the decadence of our own society?

Of course we can do something about Marxism and its advocates. We can expose their shallowness and barbarism through every medium available to us, including books. We can give clandestine support to any group striving to throw off the Marxist yoke. We can continue to cast the light of truth upon that bankrupt philosophy and require that its apologists acknowledge the truth.

Commenting on his play *Night and Day*, Tom Stoppard underscored this point most succinctly when he wrote:

> People are so clever that, paradoxically, they can be persuaded of almost anything. For example, if one were to say to an intelligent child the following: "Life in East Germany is very agreeable, and there's a wall around it to keep people in," the child would say, "There's something wrong here." But if you said it to a professor of political science, or political history, you'd have a much better chance of persuading him that what you said isn't nonsensical.

OPEN LETTER TO A SOVIET CITIZEN

In our own Declaration of Independence, Thomas Jefferson wrote: "These colonies are, and of a right ought to be, free and independent states." Shouldn't the same right extend to the subjects of the world's only remaining great empire, the Union of Soviet Socialist Republics? Why shouldn't the colonies of Estonia, Latvia, Lithuania, Poland, Hungary, Czechoslovakia, Romania, the Ukraine, Kazakstan, Turkmenistan, Uzbekistan, Armenia, Georgia, other smaller states, and now, Afghanistan, have a right to choose their governments?

All the world knows the horror of Marxist governments. We have the witness of history since the first was created. We also have the witness of Alexander Solzhenitsyn, who returned from the living death of the slave labor camps that are essential to a Marxist government. Solzhenitsyn so thoroughly documented the systematic torture and barbarism of these camps that no reasonable, fair-minded person ever again can apologize for the political system that makes such inhumanity possible.

And so, my Soviet friend, we have our government and you have yours. Nevertheless, we pledge not to forget. We pledge to do what we can to diminish the influence of those who endorse, protect, and give comfort to your oppressors. We pledge to you the continued pursuit of truth. And, finally, we pledge to do everything in our power to help make you free.

MILBURN CALHOUN
Publisher
Pelican Publishing Company

Foreword

In 1974, I contributed the introduction to a volume prepared by the editors of the Foreign Policy Association, entitled *A Cartoon History of United States Foreign Policy*. I did not at the time understand that I was contributing—in a minor way and only unwittingly it is true—to what diplomats call an international incident.

Indeed, more than four years later, the second Moscow International Book Fair opened on September 4, 1979. American publishers arrived to the discovery that Soviet customs officers had confiscated forty-four books the preceding day. Among them was that very same *Cartoon History*. To be sure, a collection of essays by George Orwell had also been seized, and the "responsible" Soviet official described the seizure in wholly Orwellian terms.

"It is not correct to say," remarked Boris I. Stukalin, chairman of the Soviet's State Publishing Committee, "that this is a violation of freedom of speech. It is the highest affirmation of freedom of speech."

It may be that I am about to establish myself in an ongoing tradition. For Mr. Stukalin's dictum has extended even into this enterprise: no fewer than five earlier volumes in this series were removed from the same publishers' exhibition. Is it not to be anticipated that the present volume, *Best Editorial Cartoons of the Year*, 1980 Edition, will meet a similar fate when its publishers seek to exhibit it at the Moscow book fair? So if there be no other value to this new compilation of America's best editorial cartoons, let the reader examine it closely to learn precisely what it is that makes the government of a presumed superpower tremble.

What might that be? Only, perhaps, that the seeming irreverence of the cartoonist is in fact the highest respect for the democratic system which has nourished his art. Perhaps, too, a totally relaxed art form which nonetheless nourishes more than a bit of healthy disrespect for pretense and pomposity. One will find in these pages nothing but wit and ingenuity, little except that characteristic American response to dogma. One can then understand why tyrannical regimes will resist the circulation among their peoples of such self-confident expression. Indeed, the Soviets have taken the point, for there are few things more subversive than humor, few arts more menacing than humble satire. We are thus engaged in commerce of sorts: it is America's task to prepare these volumes, and it is the task of the Stukalins of the world to be shaken by them.

Yet we know that the political cartoon would not be so firmly established in our culture if its sole purpose were ridicule. We find in

FOREWORD

our best cartoons something more even than incisive social commentary—namely a repeated call for civic honesty. The editorials in our press offer analysis and argument, but the cartoons on the same page set forth an almost instinctual standard against which the behavior of government can be measured.

More reliable than any poll, they become an art which embodies a kind of received wisdom. They give us the knowledge of politics that is most worth having, and the practitioner of the political ignores it at his proverbial peril.

Here then is another volume in a series of enduring value. More than an adornment of our political culture, it is a pungent and appealing reminder of those things that make us what we are.

DANIEL PATRICK MOYNIHAN
United States Senator
New York

PAUL SZEP
Courtesy Boston Globe

10

Award-Winning Cartoons

1979 PULITZER PRIZE*
*(Selected by Pulitzer Prize Editorial Board)

BOB ENGLEHART
Editorial Cartoonist
Dayton Journal Herald

Born Fort Wayne, Indiana, November 7, 1945; attended American Academy of Art; staff cartoonist, *Chicago Today*, 1966-72; editorial cartoonist, *Fort Wayne Journal Gazette*, 1972-75; editorial cartoonist, *Dayton Journal Herald*, 1975 to present; author of *Never Let Facts Get in the Way of a Good Cartoon!*, 1979; honored with awards from the U.S. Industrial Council, the U.N. Population Institute, and the Overseas Press Club; syndicated by the Copley News Service.

1978 SIGMA DELTA CHI AWARD
(Selected in 1979)

JIM BORGMAN
Editorial Cartoonist
Cincinnati Enquirer

Born in Cincinnati, Ohio, February 24, 1954; B.A. with honors, Kenyon College, 1976; Phi Beta Kappa; Summa Cum Laude; awarded Art Prize as Outstanding Art Student of the Year, 1976; winner of E. Malcolm Anderson Cup, 1976; staff artist and editorial cartoonist for the *Kenyon Collegian*, 1974-76; editorial cartoonist, *Cincinnati Enquirer*, 1976 to present; syndicated by King Features.

TERRY MOSHER
(AISLIN)
Editorial Cartoonist
Montreal Gazette

Born in Ottawa, Ontario, 1942; attended Central Technical School, Toronto, 1961-63, Ontario College of Art, 1963-64, L'Ecole des Beaux-Arts, 1965-66; staff cartoonist for the *Montreal Star*, 1969-71; art director, *Take One* magazine, 1970 to present; staff cartoonist, Montreal Gazette, 1972 to present; cartoons syndicated by Toronto Star Syndicate; uses pen name "Aislin," his daughter's name; previously won National Newspaper Award, 1977.

Best Editorial Cartoons of the Year

Soviet Book-Banning

Five volumes of the annual series *Best Editorial Cartoons of the Year* were confiscated by Russian authorities at the second annual Moscow International Book Fair in September.

A total of 44 books of some 13,000 displayed by American publishers were removed from the exhibit hall, unleashing a storm of protest from the American literary world. Many publishers, who had submitted books at the request of Soviet authorities, indicated they would decline to participate in future book fairs in Russia.

Russian officials brazenly dismissed the charge that censorship was involved. In a bizarre twist of logic, a Soviet spokesman announced that the book-banning "represents the highest affirmation of freedom of speech."

Soviet authorities said that the volumes of *Best Editorial Cartoons of the Year* portrayed the Russian system of government in an unfavorable light.

"OUT!"

CHARLES BROOKS
Courtesy Birmingham (Ala.) News

JACK McLEOD
Courtesy Buffalo Evening News

SOVIET BOOK WORM

HY ROSEN
Courtesy Albany Times-Union

Presidential Candidates

The presidential campaign was well under way long before 1980, and it heated up early. The prevailing theory seemed to be that it was impossible to begin too early—particularly since Jimmy Carter had campaigned for two years to win the presidency.

Rep. Philip Crane of Illinois may have set an early-bird record when he announced on August 2, 1978, that he would seek the Republican nomination in 1980. By year's end he had already campaigned in forty-five states, with thirty-five visits to New Hampshire and thirty-two to Florida. John Connally of Texas declared his candidacy on January 24, 1979, and was the top money raiser with more than $6 million in his treasury.

Other Republican candidates were Ronald Reagan, who was widely regarded as the front-runner; Sen. Howard Baker of Tennessee; former United Nations Ambassador George Bush, who spent much of the year campaigning in Iowa; Sen. Robert Dole of Kansas; and Rep. John Anderson of Illinois. Former President Gerald Ford was standing in the wings, ready to step on stage as a compromise candidate if the voters beckoned.

On the Democrat side, Sen. Edward M. Kennedy and California Governor Jerry Brown represented President Carter's major challengers.

A total of 112 men and women had announced as candidates for president by the end of the year.

ROBERT GRAYSMITH
Courtesy San Francisco Chronicle

BOB TAYLOR
Courtesy Dallas Times Herald

STEVE GREENBERG
*Courtesy Valley News,
Van Nuys, Cal.*

KARL HUBENTHAL
*Courtesy Los Angeles
Herald-Examiner*

"Jerry Brown!"

JIM BERRY
©NEA

Not Funny Anymore

1980 PRESIDENTIAL ELECTION

LIBERAL TRUDEAU UPSET IN CANADA

CONSERVATIVE MARGARET THATCHER WINS IN BRITAIN

EDDIE GERMANO
Courtesy Brockton Daily Enterprise

FRANK EVERS
Courtesy N. Y. Daily News

TOM CURTIS
Courtesy Milwaukee Sentinel

JIM BORGMAN
Courtesy Cincinnati Enquirer

Carter Administration

President Carter's approval rating during 1979 dropped lower in the polls than for any other president since poll-taking began. At midyear nearly three of every four Americans disapproved of the way Carter was performing his job, according to a *New York Times*-CBS poll.

The president's own pollster urged Carter to change his image to one of boldness and decisive action. Shortly thereafter, Carter staged a sweeping shake-up of his cabinet and White House personnel, firing five cabinet members and installing Hamilton Jordan as chief of staff. The president also took a much-publicized trip down the Mississippi River aboard the *Delta Queen*.

Andrew Young was forced to resign as United Nations ambassador after he was found to have lied about a meeting with the Palestine Liberation Organization. The resignation caused widespread anger among black supporters of Carter.

In September, Carter said that the presence of a newly discovered Soviet brigade in Cuba was "unacceptable," but the Russians declined to remove them and the president decided he could live with the situation.

The Carter Administration's most difficult problem erupted in November when Iranian leftists captured the American embassy and held some sixty Americans hostage. At year's end some fifty were still captive.

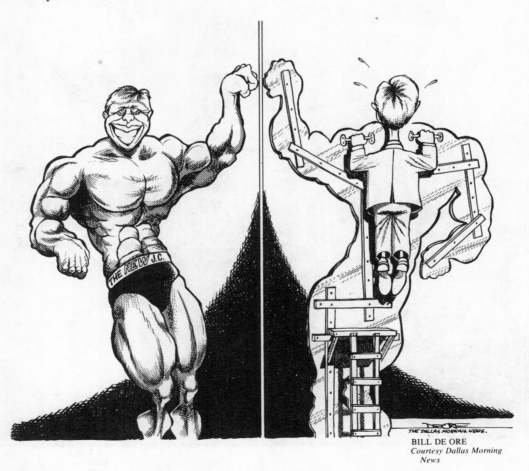

BILL DE ORE
Courtesy Dallas Morning News

BOAT PEOPLE!

SHIP OF STAT

CABINET CASUALTIES

ADRIFT!

HERC FICKLEN

HERC FICKLEN
©Avalon Features

JOHN BRANCH
Courtesy Chapel Hill News

THE CHAPEL HILL NEWSPAPER

GUIDELINE INN

FRANK EVERS

FRANK EVERS
Courtesy N. Y. Daily News

GENE BASSET
Courtesy Scripps-Howard Newspapers

LEE JUDGE
Courtesy San Diego Union

DICK WRIGHT
*Courtesy Providence
Journal-Bulletin*

THE Inner circle

DOUG SNEYD
©Sneyd Syndicate

CRAIG MACINTOSH
Courtesy Minneapolis Star

KEN ALEXANDER
Courtesy San Francisco Examiner

GENE BASSET
Courtesy Scripps-Howard Newspapers

"THIS IS YOUR LEADER REPORTING FROM HIS BUNKER ... TO RESTORE PUBLIC CONFIDENCE AND PURGE THE DISLOYAL, I HAVE PROMOTED HAMILTON JORDAN TO FIELD MARSHAL."

RAOUL HUNTER
Courtesy Le Soleil (Quebec)

JACK JURDEN
Courtesy Wilmington
News-Journal

AT THE HALFWAY POST!

"This is ANOTHER fine mess you've gotten us into!"

JIM BERRY
©NEA

JIM DOBBINS
Courtesy Manchester
Union-Leader

BLAINE
Courtesy The Spectator, Canada

DRAPER HILL
Courtesy Detroit News

MARK TAYLOR
Courtesy Albuquerque Tribune

THE GALLUP HOLE

SCOTT LONG
Courtesy Minneapolis Tribune

CHARLES WERNER
Courtesy Indianapolis Star

"GO AHEAD AND DIVE IN — ROSALYNN SAYS IT'S BRIMMING FULL!"

CHARLES BROOKS
Courtesy Birmingham (Ala.) News

ART BIMROSE
Courtesy Portland Oregonian

BOB ENGLEHART
Courtesy Dayton Journal Herald

REG MANNING
Courtesy Arizona Republic

CHESTER COMMODORE
Courtesy Chicago Daily Defender

BRIAN BASSET
Courtesy Seattle Times

AL LIEDERMAN
©Rothco

32

CLYDE WELLS
Courtesy Augusta (Ga.) Chronicle

TOM CURTIS
Courtesy Milwaukee Sentinel

Senator Kennedy

Forty-seven-year-old Sen. Edward M. Kennedy on November 7 finally made the long-anticipated announcement that he would be a candidate for the presidency in the 1980 election. After making his declaration in Boston at historic Faneuil Hall, he opened a frantic five-day tour. The tour took him to eight cities, where he was met with enthusiasm in some quarters and cold hostility in others. He attacked President Carter repeatedly, charging a lack of leadership.

The Chappaquiddick issue lingered on, and Kennedy went on national television again in an attempt to deal with the problem. The consensus was that his rambling, almost incoherent answers to an interviewer's questions damaged his campaign seriously, perhaps fatally.

In any event, the much-heralded Kennedy campaign for the presidency was slow to get off the ground.

BOB GORRELL
Courtesy Fort Myers
News-Press

TIMOTHY ATSEFF
Syracuse Herald-Journal
©Richmond Syndicate

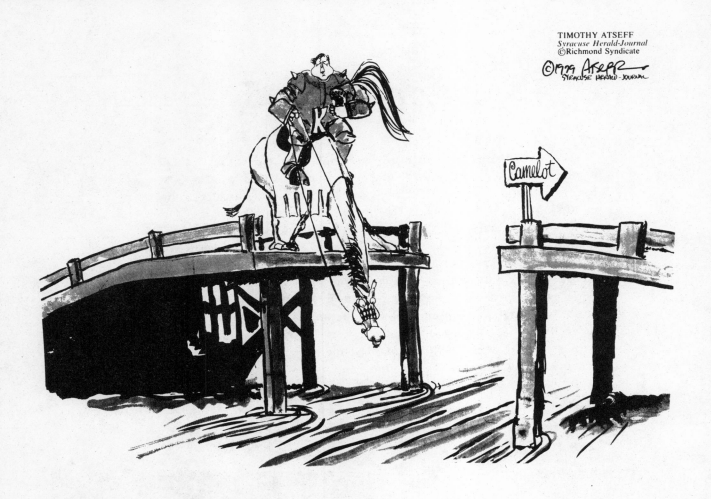

TOM CURTIS
Courtesy Milwaukee Sentinel

BRIAN BASSET
Courtesy Seattle Times

CHARLES DANIEL
Courtesy Knoxville Journal

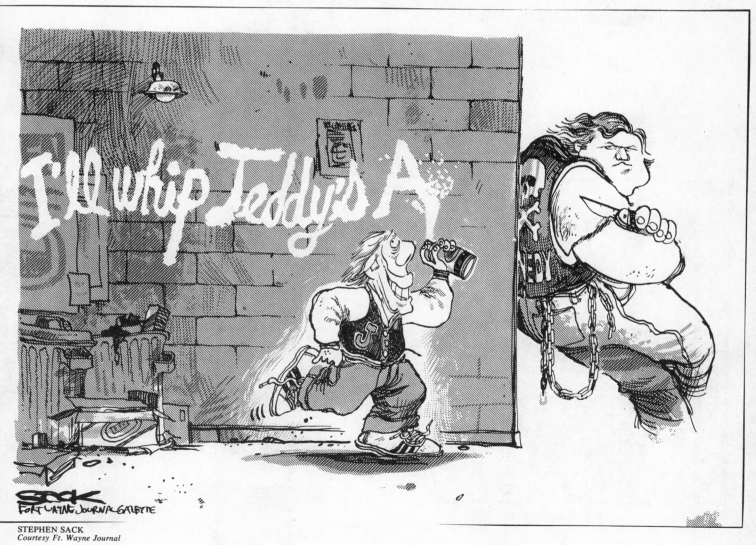

STEPHEN SACK
Courtesy Ft. Wayne Journal

ED GAMBLE
Courtesy Nashville Banner

ART HENRIKSON
©Paddock Publications

Ted Kennedy officially mounts presidential campaign

I wish I could count sheep!

PAUL SZEP
Courtesy Boston Globe

I AM A CANDIDATE FOR PRESIDENT...

...SO WE CAN HAVE A DYNAMIC FOREIGN POLICY...

...AN EFFICIENT ENERGY PROGRAM...

...WITHOUT INFLATION...

...WITHOUT POVERTY...

...AND WITH STRONG LEADERSHIP

WELL...UH...UH...A...A...UH, UH...A.....

HOW?

GENE BASSET
Courtesy Scripps-Howard Newspapers

BOSTON TEA PARTY

ED FISCHER
Courtesy Omaha World-Herald

DANA SUMMERS
*Courtesy Fayetteville
(N. C.) Times*

RICHARD CROWSON
Courtesy Jackson (Tenn.) Sun

PATRICK CROWLEY
*Courtesy West Palm Beach
Post*

Iran and the Mideast

World attention focused upon Iran throughout most of the year, with turmoil, violence, and bloodshed the recurring elements. The revolutionary Islamic regime of Ayatollah Khomeini launched deadly reprisals against fellow countrymen who had been allied with the deposed shah, executing hundreds.

The new regime was strongly anti-American, berating the United States and its president almost daily. Then, the unthinkable happened. A horde of revolutionaries seized the U.S. embassy in Teheran and took some sixty Americans hostage. They vowed the hostages would not be freed until the shah, who was in New York for special medical treatment, was returned to Iran to stand trial for alleged crimes.

Several women and black hostages were released, but efforts to gain freedom for the remaining fifty or so proved futile. Meanwhile, the shah left the U.S. and set up residence in Panama.

Israel and Egypt finally concluded the peace treaty that had been worked out many months before at Camp David. President Carter flew to the Middle East and after several days of shuttle diplomacy between Cairo and Jerusalem, resolved the remaining areas of disagreement and obtained the treaty signatures.

IRANIAN BIRD OF PRAY

PAUL SZEP
Courtesy Boston Globe

ROY PETERSON
Courtesy Vancouver Sun

"It only hurts when I leave . . . ."

HY ROSEN
Courtesy Albany Times-Union

"HELLO, I'M PUTTING THE WORLD ON TRIAL!"

PREPARING THE KOOLADE!

CHARLES WERNER
Courtesy Indianapolis Star

DRAPER HILL
Courtesy Detroit News

VIC ROSCHKOV
Courtesy Toronto Star

JEFF MACNELLY
Richmond News Leader
©Chicago Tribune—New York
News Syndicate

KEN ALEXANDER
Courtesy San Francisco Examiner

THE FOREIGN GUEST ABUSING THE SANCTITY OF HIS HOST

VERN THOMPSON
Courtesy Lawton (Okla.) Constitution

FRANK INTERLANDI
©Los Angeles Times Syndicate

BERT WHITMAN
Courtesy Phoenix Gazette

HOLY ISLAMIC COURT IN SESSION

ED ULUSCHAK
Courtesy Edmonton (Can.) Journal

"It was making music"

BOB ARTLEY
Courtesy Worthington (Minn.) Daily Globe

MARK TAYLOR
Courtesy Albuquerque
Tribune

ROY PETERSON
Courtesy Vancouver Sun

TIM MENEES
*Courtesy Pittsburgh
Post-Gazette*

BILL GARNER
Courtesy The Commercial Appeal

MIKE PETERS
Courtesy Dayton Daily News

RAY OSRIN
Courtesy Cleveland Plain Dealer

"STEP ASIDE, AMATEUR!"

PAUL DUGINSKI
Courtesy Sacramento Union

DICK WALLMEYER
Long Beach Press-Telegram
©Register and Tribune Syndicate

SANDY CAMPBELL
Courtesy The Tennessean

ROGER HARVELL
*Courtesy Pine Bluff (Ark.)
Commercial*

SIGN HERE!

EGYPT

SIGN HERE!

ISRAEL

I DIDN'T KNOW POLITICAL SURVIVAL WAS SO STRENUOUS!

FRANK INTERLANDI
©Los Angeles Times Syndicate

XI
Thou shalt continue to expand thy settlements even onto the Left Bank.

JERRY ROBINSON
©Cartoonists and Writers Snydicate

BEN WICKS
Courtesy Toronto Sun

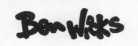

'Sure I like you best, Anwar. But then again, I like Menahem best too!'

PRESS CORPS

MIDEAST STORY

BALDY
Courtesy Atlanta Constitution
Baldy

" ... PEACE ? ... DAMN, Jody, YOU PROMISED US A WAR!"

DENNIS RENAULT
Courtesy Sacramento Bee

ETTA HULME
Courtesy Ft. Worth Star-Telegram

"They're obviously terrorists. One is threatening me with his fist right now!"

CRAIG MACINTOSH
Courtesy Minneapolis Star

'Not a bad day, sir. We got two PLO jeeps, a terrorist ammo dump, a weapons cache, a dozen direct hits on Tyre and Andy Young'

Energy

Long lines at the gasoline pumps across America brought home once again the fact that America's energy problem shows no sign of going away. Panic buying of gasoline started on the West Coast in early May after supplies became tight. California's Governor Jerry Brown came up with an even-odd license plan to enable motorists to buy gasoline only on correspondingly even or odd days of the month.

The California panic spread across the country and seemed to hit the populous Northeast hardest of all. Causes of the shortage were complex, but most consumers placed the blame on the federal allocation system.

The revolution in Iran caused a reduction in oil shipments to America early in the year, and after leftists seized the U.S. embassy in Teheran in November, President Carter ordered an immediate halt to all imports from Iran.

Global supply and demand caused a steady hike in the cost of gasoline, with unleaded gas selling at year's end for more than $1 per gallon, a jump of about 30 cents per gallon during 1979.

A blowout of an oil well owned by the government of Mexico poured more than three million barrels into the Gulf of Mexico in June. The largest oil spill in history, it fouled waters along the coast of Texas, and the Mexican government refused to pay for the damage.

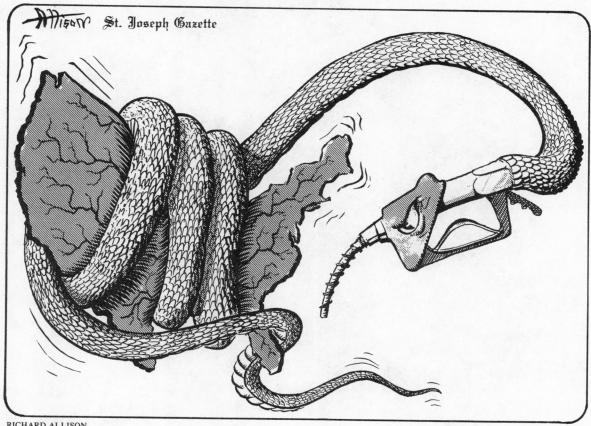

RICHARD ALLISON
Courtesy St. Joseph (Mo.)
Gazette

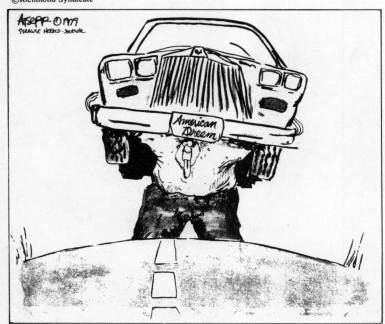

TIMOTHY ATSEFF
Syracuse Herald-Journal
©Richmond Syndicate

JERRY FEARING
Courtesy St. Paul Dispatch

BOB TAYLOR
Courtesy Dallas Times Herald

RAY OSRIN
Courtesy Cleveland Plain Dealer

BOB ENGLEHART
Courtesy Dayton Journal Herald

ED GAMBLE
Courtesy Nashville Banner

BOB SULLIVAN
Courtesy Worcester (Mass.) Telegram

ROB LAWLOR
Courtesy Philadelphia Daily News

JOHN MILT MORRIS
©The Associated Press

NEW MODEL

MARK TAYLOR
Courtesy Albuquerque Tribune

EUGENE CRAIG
Courtesy Columbus (O.) Dispatch

JACK BENDER
Waterloo Courier
©Rothco Cartoons, Inc.

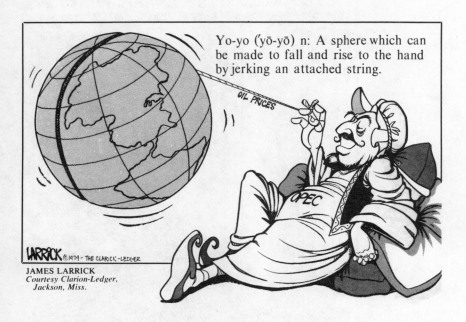

JAMES LARRICK
Courtesy Clarion-Ledger,
Jackson, Miss.

LEW HARSH
Courtesy Scranton Times

ED STEIN
Courtesy Rocky Mountain
News

PAUL FELL
©Maverick Media, Inc.

58

PROFIT SHARING PLAN!

JOHN MILT MORRIS
©The Associated Press

MIKE KONOPACKI
Madison Press Connection
©Rothco

PAUL DUGINSKI
Courtesy Sacramento Union

GUERNSEY LEPELLEY
Courtesy Christian Science Monitor

'You could keep warmer, ma, if you used
more insulation.'

DRILLING DEEPER

JOHN RIEDELL
Courtesy Peoria Journal

GEORGE FISHER
Courtesy Arkansas Gazette

TIM MENEES
Courtesy Pittsburgh
Post-Gazette

"ALL RIGHT, GENTLEMEN—HOW DO WE GET OUT OF THIS MESS??!!"

JIM BORGMAN
Courtesy Cincinnati Enquirer

JOHN TREVER
*Courtesy Albuquerque
Journal*

JULY 4, 1979

' I'm not quite ready '

EUGENE CRAIG
Courtesy Columbus (O.) Dispatch

FRANK EVERS
Courtesy N. Y. Daily News

IT'S ALSO FULL OF LEAD!

CHARLES WERNER
Courtesy Indianapolis Star

YE MOTORIST

EDDIE GERMANO
Courtesy Brockton Daily Enterprise

UNLEADED ONLY

GAS

STEPHEN SACK
Courtesy Ft. Wayne Journal

'JUST TOP OFF THE TANK....'

Refining The Windfall Profits Tax

'News' Item

"HUP,..TWO,...THREE...FOUR..."

—I TELL YOU... IT'S JUST ABOUT DRY!!—

ED GAMBLE
Courtesy Nashville Banner

'Fill her up. I just won a lottery!'

BEN WICKS
Courtesy Toronto Sun

"I ROAST ALL DAY IN A 78° SWEAT SHOP AND YOU WANT TO KNOW HOW MY DAY WAS?"

BILL GARNER
Courtesy The Commercial Appeal

JOHN...DID YOU TURN OUT THE LIGHT IN THE BATHROOM?... WE MUST REDUCE OUR STANDARD OF LIVING... YOU KNOW!

"I'll Write Every Day"
TOM FLANNERY
Courtesy Baltimore Sun

JAMES LARRICK
Courtesy Clarion-Ledger,
Jackson, Miss.

APPEASING THE ANGRY SPIRITS

DICK LOCHER
Chicago Tribune
©Chicago Tribune—N.Y.
News Syndicate

"NO, YOU OPEN IT !"

LET'S FACE THE MUSIC!

HERC FICKLEN
©Avalon Features

VIC RUNTZ
Courtesy Bangor Daily News

"Don't get us wrong, Mexico! It's not that we don't
want your oil, but . . . ."

ALL RIGHT, FELLA, HOW MUCH HAS THAT CAR HAD TO DRINK ?!

HIC

JIM PALMER
Courtesy Montgomery
Advertiser

China

On January 1, 1979, the U.S. established formal diplomatic relations with the People's Republic of China—nearly thirty years after the communists took over the government. Thus, President Carter abandoned Taiwan, a longtime ally, for newly found friends.

It was announced that the U.S. would maintain "cultural, commercial, and other unofficial relations" with the Taiwanese, and the sale of arms was to continue, even after normalization with Peking.

The major factors in the new breakthrough in Sino-American relations were a mutual interest in expanding trade and economic relations and a growing concern over Russian influence in Asia.

Chinese Deputy Premier Deng Xiaoping (Teng Hsiao-ping) arrived in the U.S. in January for a nine-day visit, receiving a warm reception in most areas. Corporate interests were anxious to engage in business with China, and Coca-Cola was the first to tap the vast new market with orders in hand.

ETTA HULME
Courtesy Ft. Worth Star-Telegram

JERRY ROBINSON
©Cartoonists and Writers
Snydicate

MERLE TINGLEY
Courtesy London (Can.) Free Press

DICK WALLMEYER
Long Beach Press-Telegram
©Register and Tribune Syndicate

JERRY ROBINSON
©Cartoonists and Writers
Snydicate

TERRY MOSHER (AISLIN)
Courtesy Montreal Gazette

JIM DOBBINS
*Courtesy Manchester
Union-Leader*

I DON'T KNOW WHAT GOT INTO ME.... I WENT TO AMERICA.... I ATE HAMBURGERS AND DRANK COKA COLA.... I WORE A TEN GALLON HAT, AND THEN I INVADED VIETNAM ...

BURNING THE MIDNIGHT OIL

Salt II and Russia

After seven years of negotiations between the U.S. and the Soviet Union, President Carter and Leonid Brezhnev on June 18 initialed a second Strategic Arms Limitation Treaty. The two leaders also signed a series of agreed-upon statements and understandings pertaining to the obligations of each party.

The aim of Salt II is to set limits on stockpiling nuclear weapons, thus slowing the nuclear arms race. It also is intended to set limits on delivery systems.

Under the U.S. Constitution, Senate approval is required to ratify a treaty. On June 9 the Senate opened hearings on ratification in the Foreign Relations Committee. There was much doubt in the committee over the treaty's verification process—that is, whether the U.S. would be able to determine if the Soviets were living up to their end of the bargain.

The discovery of Russian combat troops in Cuba near the end of 1979 was a severe setback to ratification. Then, at year's end, Russia's invasion of Afghanistan apparently sealed Salt II's doom. President Carter realized it would not pass and asked that the hearings be delayed.

DAN ADAMS
Courtesy Hillsboro, Ore.,
Argus

PATRICK CROWLEY
Courtesy West Palm Beach
Post

BURIAL PROCESS

DON HESSE
Courtesy St. Louis Globe-Democrat

RICHARD ALLISON
Courtesy St. Joseph (Mo.)
Gazette

SCOTT LONG
Courtesy Minneapolis Tribune

74

TOM CURTIS
Courtesy Milwaukee Sentinel

"I'm going to have to ask you not to cheat!"

JEFF MACNELLY
Richmond News Leader
©Chicago Tribune—New York
News Syndicate

ED ASHLEY
Courtesy Toledo Blade

WAYNE STAYSKAL
Courtesy Chicago Tribune

A NIGHT AT THE BOLSHOI

DICK LOCHER
Chicago Tribune
©Chicago Tribune—N.Y.
News Syndicate

BERT WHITMAN
Courtesy Phoenix Gazette

JOHN STAMPONE
Courtesy Army Times

77

ED ULUSCHAK
Courtesy Edmonton (Can.) Journal

ED ASHLEY
Courtesy Toledo Blade

U. S. Economy

America's gross national product (adjusted for inflation) held stationary during 1979. Normal growth rate is about 3 percent. In a broad range of industries both production and jobs declined.

Automakers wound up the year in serious trouble, with all having to lay off workers and cut back production. In mid-October the three biggest manufacturers unveiled their 1980 models, expecting a jump in sales. For the following ten days, however, new car sales dropped 7 percent below 1978 levels.

Chrysler's financial problems created the big economic news. The giant company was expected to lose $1 billion for the year and faced bankruptcy without government assistance. Congress passed bail-out legislation guaranteeing Chrysler $1.5 billion in loans while requiring $462.5 million in contract concessions from the company's 113,000 union workers.

U.S. airlines laid off hundreds of workers, cut back on flights, and delayed expansion plans as earnings dipped because of the rising cost of jet fuel. Their monthly fuel bills increased by $300 million during the year.

U.S. Steel, too, had its problems, laying off some 13,000 employees and shutting down sixteen plants that were losing money.

At year's end, the inflation rate stood at 13.5 percent, with unemployment running at 5.8 percent.

1980 MODEL

KARL HUBENTHAL
Courtesy Los Angeles
Herald-Examiner

THE CRASH OF '79

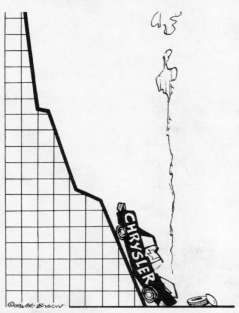

ART BIMROSE
Courtesy Portland Oregonian

JIMMY JOHNSON
Courtesy Jackson (Miss.)
Daily News

Johnson JACKSON DAILY NEWS

"I'M YOUR NEW PHYSICIAN"

ED FISCHER
Courtesy Omaha World-Herald

SOME BANKS OUT OF MORTGAGE MONEY — NEWS ITEM

CLYDE PETERSON
Courtesy Houston Chronicle

1979 Register & Tribune Syndicate

'Blessed be the takers of obscene losses for theirs shall be
the obscene tax bucks'

80

GENE BASSET
Courtesy Scripps-Howard Newspapers

"YOU MAY BE WONDERING WHY I CALLED YOU HERE. WELL, WE'RE ORGANIZING A BAIL OUT SQUAD"

DICK LOCHER
Chicago Tribune
©Chicago Tribune—N.Y.
News Syndicate

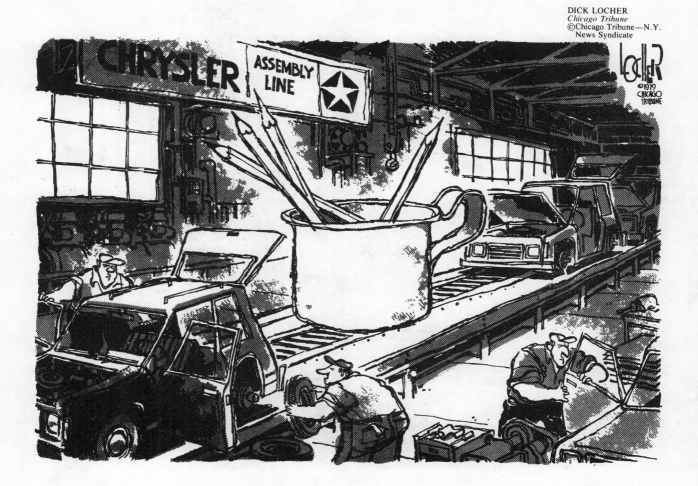

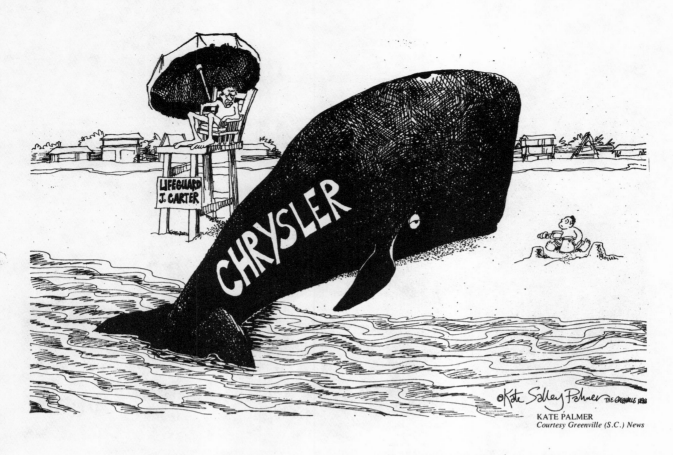

KATE PALMER
Courtesy Greenville (S.C.) News

DAN ADAMS
*Courtesy Hillsboro, Ore.,
Argus*

"IT'S A BRAND-NEW ENGINEERING IDEA ... OPERATES ON
HIGH-OCTANE FEDERAL SUPPORT!"

'LOOKS LIKE THE FED RELEASED ANOTHER REPORT...'

ED FISCHER
Courtesy Omaha World-Herald

LEONARD NORRIS
Courtesy Vancouver (Can.) Sun

"... next, I'll work out the total interest over the 25-year mortgage, which may cause you some raised eyebrows ...."

ED ULUSCHAK
Courtesy Edmonton (Can.) Journal

"Oh, oh — I don't like the looks of this."

JAMES LARRICK
*Courtesy Clarion-Ledger,
Jackson, Miss.*

Inflation

Inflation continued to climb apace, soaring to an annual rate of 13.2 percent for the year. While the price spiral was expected to continue for the next several years, the business community expressed concern about the possibility of recession amid inflation. Americans seemed resigned to a future in which prices would rise from 10 to 13 percent in each of the next several years.

In a bold move to subdue inflation, the Federal Reserve Board on October 6 ordered a tightening of credit, driving the prime borrowing rate above 16 percent. Many citizens unwittingly helped to fuel inflation by borrowing money to speculate in property, gold, jewelry, and other goods that might hold their value.

The escalating cost of energy contributed substantially to inflation, with oil prices increasing a whopping 60 percent. Home purchase prices rose 16 percent as interest rates skyrocketed.

MIKE KEEFE
Courtesy Denver Post

STEPHEN SACK
Courtesy Ft. Wayne Journal

ECLIPSE

ART WOOD
Courtesy Farm Bureau News

ELDON PLETCHER
New Orleans Times-Picayune
©Rothco

JACK BENDER
Waterloo Courier
©Rothco Cartoons, Inc.

ELDON PLETCHER
New Orleans Times-Picayune
©Rothco

ED ASHLEY
Courtesy Toledo Blade

JERRY FEARING
Courtesy St. Paul Dispatch

A WOMAN SCORNED

JIM LANGE
The Daily Oklahoman
©The Oklahoma Publishing Co.

"ACTUALLY IT TURNED OUT OKAY, MR. SWANEY. I GAVE HIM ALL THOSE SUSAN ANTHONY DOLLAR COINS NOBODY ELSE WILL TAKE!"

DOUG SNEYD
©Sneyd Syndicate

88

LEONARD NORRIS
Courtesy Vancouver (Can.) Sun

"One day, my lads, all these will be yours . . . ."

CLYDE PETERSON
Courtesy Houston Chronicle

KATE PALMER
Courtesy Greenville (S.C.) News

LARRY WRIGHT
Courtesy Detroit News

'Why is it that whenever we meet, all you seem to think about is inflation?'

BEN WICKS
Courtesy Toronto Sun

"High-o Silver, away!"

VIC RUNTZ
Courtesy Bangor Daily News

MIKE KEEFE
Courtesy Denver Post

Congress and Bureaucracy

During the year Congress gave President Carter its approval of a new Washington bureaucracy—a Department of Education, consisting of some 17,000 employees and an annual budget of $14.2 billion. After having debated the matter for years, the House of Representatives finally permitted live broadcasts of its sessions.

For the first time since 1921 a member of the House, Rep. Charles C. Diggs, Jr. (D-Mich.), was censured. A federal court had convicted him of misusing his government payroll. The Senate, after much study, followed the recommendation of its ethics committee, voting to "denounce" Sen. Herman Talmadge (D-Ga.) for "gross neglect of duty" and for peculiar financial computations that brought "dishonor and disrepute" to the Senate.

Three persons indicted in the General Services Administration scandal pleaded guilty to taking kickbacks from private contractors. Other cases of bribery, payoffs, and conspiracy in the GSA came to light as others pleaded guilty to various charges. It was determined that widespread stealing by GSA employees had been taking place for several years.

DANA SUMMERS
Courtesy Fayetteville
(N. C.) Times

'YOU POUR AND I'LL FLUSH'

DON HESSE
Courtesy St. Louis Globe-Democrat

PLEASE... MY PROBLEM NEEDS A PERSON!

JIM ORTON
©Computer World

"... YOU MAY WONDER WHY I CALLED THIS STAFF MEETING!"

BALDY
Courtesy Atlanta Constitution

Mr. Potato-Head

KATE PALMER
Courtesy Greenville (S.C.) News

TOM ENGELHARDT
Courtesy St. Louis Post-Dispatch

'Not Now, Jimmy — I'm In A Re-Election Race'

WAYNE STAYSKAL
Courtesy Chicago Tribune

"I HOPE YOU REALIZE, SIR, THAT IF YOU WERE A MEMBER OF THE HOUSE OF REPRESENTATIVES YOU'D BE CENSURED FOR THIS!"

DON HESSE
Courtesy St. Louis Globe-Democrat

ART WOOD
Courtesy Farm Bureau News

ART POINIER
© United Feature Syndicate

GEORGE FISHER
Courtesy Arkansas Gazette

Foreign Relations

The prestige of the United States around the world sank lower during 1979 than at any previous time since its birth. American flags were ripped down from many U.S. embassies, U.S. installations were stoned, and crowds stormed other American buildings abroad.

The ultimate insult, of course, was reached when Iranian militants occupied the U.S. embassy in Teheran on November 4. The rioting mob seized some sixty Americans and held them hostage.

As the year progressed, President Carter seemed to move toward National Security Advisor Zbigniew Brzezinski's hardline approach to Russia—but only slightly. Through much of the year the softliners— Secretary of State Cyrus Vance, Defense Secretary Harold Brown, and United Nations Ambassador Andrew Young—held the President's ear.

In September the President backed down on a pledge to compel the Soviet Union to remove a brigade of troops from Cuba.

All in all, American prestige declined throughout the world.

JEFF MACNELLY
Richmond News Leader
©Chicago Tribune—New York
News Syndicate.

HY ROSEN
Courtesy Albany Times-Union

"THE RUSSIANS AREN'T COMING! THE RUSSIANS AREN'T COMING!"

KARL HUBENTHAL
*Courtesy Los Angeles
Herald-Examiner*

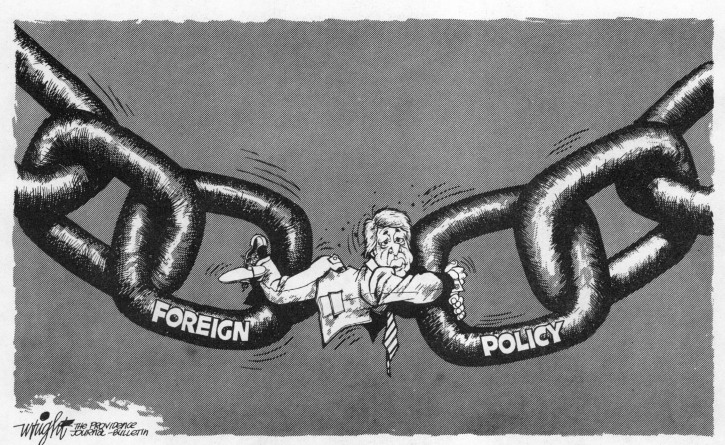

DICK WRIGHT
*Courtesy Providence
Journal-Bulletin*

a chain is only as strong as its weakest link

ROB LAWLOR
Courtesy Philadelphia Daily News

S. C. RAWLS
Courtesy Palm Beach Post

BOB SULLIVAN
Courtesy Worcester Telegram

HUGH HAYNIE
Louisville Courier-Journal
©Los Angeles Times Syndicate

"It'll be tough to replace a man of your caliber, Andy, ol' buddy."

A CRISES OF CONFIDENCE!

ED FISCHER
Courtesy Omaha World-Herald

THE L. A. TIMES SYNDICATE

"Now, listen . . . I am rapidly running out of cheeks to turn . . . !"

HUGH HAYNIE
Louisville Courier-Journal
©Los Angeles Times Syndicate

98

Courts and the Press

Freedom of the press was eroded in a variety of cases during the year. Press protection in libel suits was narrowed as the U.S. Supreme Court reconsidered its definition and application of a "public figure" in modern society.

In one case, the Court held that the First Amendment does not protect the pre-publication or pre-broadcast thoughts, conversations, or conclusions of reporters or editors from anyone suing for libel. In another case, it ruled that a person does not become a public figure simply by committing a criminal act or being involved in an event that attracts public attention.

The Supreme Court also ruled that neither the public nor the press has a constitutional right to attend pre-trial criminal hearings if the accused, the prosecutor, and the judge agree that a closed court is essential to a fair trial.

In March, a monthly magazine, *The Progressive*, was placed under a restraining order not to publish information on the workings of a hydrogen bomb. When much of the same information was later published in a small Wisconsin newspaper, the government dropped its case against *The Progressive*.

One of the most publicized stories of the year was the eleven-week trial in which actor Lee Marvin was sued for breach of contract by a former live-in girl friend. The judge rejected her claim, but awarded her $104,000 for "reeducation."

SHACKLES ON YOUR RIGHT TO KNOW!

REDUCED LIBEL PROTECTION

RESTRICTIONS ON CRIME REPORTING

CLOSED TRIAL PRESSURE

PRESS FREEDOM

EDITORIAL THOUGHT PROBING

VERN THOMPSON
Courtesy Lawton (Okla.) Constitution

THE LAWTON CONSTITUTION

10-79

TOUCHING UP AN OLD MASTERPIECE

THE BURGER COURT

"They're writing a position paper on press freedom."

JOHN STAMPONE
Courtesy Army Times

DICK WALLMEYER
Long Beach Press-Telegram
ⒸRegister and Tribune Syndicate

THE PRESS

TYPEWRITER COVER?

ROY CARLESS
Courtesy Steelabor

"WE KNOW YOU'RE IN THERE. WE'VE GOT YOU SURROUNDED!" COME OUT WITH YOUR QUOTAS UP.

CHESTER COMMODORE
Courtesy Chicago Daily Defender

ETTA HULME
Courtesy Ft. Worth Star-Telegram

"JUST REMEMBER THE RULES — NO NOISY POWER TOOLS, AND NO ABOVE-GROUND TEST SHOTS IN THE LIBRARY"

JOHN CRAWFORD
Courtesy Alabama Journal

"HE'S GOT TIME FOR THINGS LIKE THAT.... BUT JUST ASK HIM TO FIX SOMETHING AROUND THIS HOUSE"

'I published How To Build an H Bomb to
prove we have freedom of the press.'

"Your mom and dad tell me you're building
an atomic bomb in the basement ..."

'The subscription department is down the hall'

ED STEIN
*Courtesy Rocky Mountain
News*

LARRY WRIGHT
Courtesy Detroit News

The Boat People

On November 9, 1978, an ancient, nearly worn-out freighter, the *Hai Hong*, limped into Kuala Lumpur and asked permission to unload its cargo of 2,500 Vietnamese refugees. Virtually all of them suffered from sickness and malnutrition.

The Malaysian government, however, threatened to drive the ship back out to sea. Authorities finally agreed to provide supplies, but would allow ashore only those who had been accepted for permanent residence in other countries.

Thus, the world's attention focused upon one of history's most tragic stories.

Other ships laden with refugees were turned away from other Asian ports, often by force, and repulsing refugees seemed to be official policy in much of that region of the world. Furthermore, refugee boats were often ignored by passing ships, while others fell prey to pirate ships. During the first half of 1979, some 50,000 persons looking for asylum in Malaysia were towed to sea and left to drown.

The war in Cambodia forced some 40,000 refugees to seek sanctuary in Thailand, but Thai troops forced most of them back across the border into Cambodia.

By midyear, approximately 220,000 Indo-Chinese refugees had been accepted into the United States, and other nations welcomed nearly 100,000.

BALDY
Courtesy Atlanta Constitution

"...NOT ANY MORE! WE'RE WORKING ON BIGGER THINGS FOR THE COUNTRY NOW!"

LEONARD NORRIS
Courtesy Vancouver (Can.) Sun

"Beset by this crisis . . . people should try to take no unnecessary trips, use car pools or public transportation whenever you can, park your car one extra day per week, obey the speed limit, and set your thermostats to save fuel . . . there is absolutely no way to avoid sacrifice." —President Carter

Raft of the Medusa, 1979

CRAIG MACINTOSH
Courtesy Minneapolis Star

BOB TAYLOR
Courtesy Dallas Times Herald

CLYDE PETERSON
Courtesy Houston Chronicle

THE REAL 'IMMORALITY' OF VIETNAM

DON HESSE
Courtesy St. Louis Globe-Democrat

'Lucky I'm around or these decadent devils would have you right in their grasp'

Holocaust, 1979

BILL GRAHAM
Courtesy Arkansas Gazette

JACK McLEOD
Courtesy Buffalo Evening News

VIETNAM PROTESTERS—1979

Aid, communist style

BOB ARTLEY
Courtesy Worthington (Minn.) Daily Globe

BOAT PEOPLE

JERRY BARNETT
Courtesy Indianapolis News

ANDY DONATO
Courtesy Toronto Sun

CLOSED SOCIETY

ED STEIN
*Courtesy Rocky Mountain
News*

ART BIMROSE
Courtesy Portland Oregonian

JOHN HIGGINS
Courtesy Daily Northwestern,
Northwestern Univ.

DOUG SNEYD
©Sneyd Syndicate

Amtrak

The Department of Transportation ordered a 43 percent cutback in Amtrak route miles at the beginning of the year, but because of the rising cost of gasoline the carrier's business nevertheless showed a 40 percent increase.

Amtrak operated only 1,600 cars, and many of those were thirty years old. Congress voted to increase funding for capital improvements and called for fewer reductions in service. Amtrak responded by eliminating or consolidating five routes that were losing money, adding two new routes, and taking over two commuter lines from Conrail.

STEPHEN SACK
Courtesy Ft. Wayne Journal

'THIS MAY BE A BAD TIME TO TELL YOU, BUT WE'VE JUST RUN OUT OF GAS...'

KEN WESTPHAL
*Courtesy Kansas City
Star-Times*

WE'RE **FINALLY** PICKIN UP STEAM!! POUR IT ON!!!

VIC RUNTZ
Courtesy Bangor Daily News

TOM FLANNERY
Courtesy Baltimore Sun

Hear that lonesome whistle blowing

"All Aboard Before Carter Cuts Rail Service Again"

LARRY WRIGHT
Courtesy Detroit News

Waste

New regulations, issued under the authority of the Resource Conservation and Recovery Act of 1976, were initiated to better control the transportation and disposal of dangerous waste products. Under provisions of the new regulations, plants producing waste material would be held fully responsible for safe handling and transportation.

One method of disposing of such wastes is to subject them to extremely high temperatures under strictly controlled conditions. The other is by burial in landfills that would be specially secured, although few such landfills presently exist. Most states have been reluctant to become dumping grounds for dangerous wastes, and the problem of safe disposal lingered on.

MIKE PETERS
Courtesy Dayton Daily News

REMEMBER THE GOOD OLD DAYS WHEN WE ONLY HAD TO SMOKE A FEW CIGARETTES AND EAT SACCHARIN?

CHARLES BISSELL
Courtesy The Tennessean

BOB ALEXANDER
Courtesy Lawrence (Mass.) Eagle-Tribune

BOB SULLIVAN
Courtesy Worcester (Mass.) Telegram

DENNIS RENAULT
Courtesy Sacramento Bee

ROOTS

BOB BECKETT
*Courtesy Burlington County
(N. J.) Times*

The Sacramento Bee

"Someday I'll have to decide what to do with all this. . .stuff!"

THE L. A. TIMES SYNDICATE

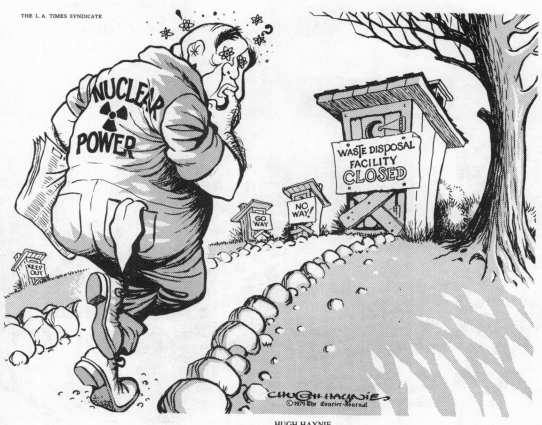

HUGH HAYNIE
Louisville Courier-Journal
©Los Angeles Times Syndicate

JOHN TREVER
Courtesy Albuquerque Journal

BLAINE
Courtesy The Spectator, Canada

JOHN CRAWFORD
Courtesy Alabama Journal

JERRY BARNETT
Courtesy Indianapolis News

JAMES MORGAN
Courtesy Spartanburg Herald-Journal

CHARLES DANIEL
Courtesy Knoxville Journal

ED ULUSCHAK
Courtesy Edmonton (Can.) Journal

"Another attempt by the media to panic the public — can you imagine the odds of being hit by a chunk of Skylab . . . Otis? . . ."

Africa

Three of the world's most heinous despots were knocked from their thrones in 1979—Idi Amin of Uganda, Macias Nguema Biyoga of Equatorial Guinea, and Emperor Bokassa of the Central African Empire. All three had squandered the treasury of their homelands and had put to death large numbers of their fellow citizens.

Amin was forced to flee Uganda after forces from neighboring Tanzania, aided by local anti-Amin groups, overran most of the country.

Biyoga was overthrown in August by his nephew, while Bokassa, who was accused of massacring dozens of high school students, was routed by a cousin backed by French troops.

In strife-torn Rhodesia, Bishop Abel Muzorewa was elected the nation's first black prime minister. A new constitution reserved twenty-eight seats in parliament for whites. Contending that the document retained too much power for former prime minister Ian Smith and his followers, British Prime Minister Margaret Thatcher met with nationalist groups and engineered a new constitution with which all parties agreed.

John B. Vorster resigned as prime minister of South Africa, and the government announced a loosening of its apartheid laws to permit blacks to hold land in white sections of the country. Black workers also were granted more freedoms.

Another angel of death is spawned

CHARLES BISSELL
Courtesy The Tennessean

VIC ROSCHKOV
Courtesy Toronto Star

GUERNSEY LEPELLEY
Courtesy Christian Science Moni

" IF ANYONE COMES ASHORE — YOU'RE ROBINSON CRUSOE AND I'M FRIDAY "

The Christian Science Mo

'On the other hand, if we don't get them down someone will start an awful fire.'

COSMETICS

SCOTT LONG
Courtesy Minneapolis Tribune

MERLE TINGLEY
Courtesy London (Can.) Free Press

DAVE GRANLUND
Courtesy Middlesex News

'MAYBE THE BEST THING TO DO IS TO WALK AWAY QUIETLY'

ED VALTMAN
©Rothco

The Pope

In the first year of his reign Pope John Paul II made three journeys outside Italy, visiting the Dominican Republic and Mexico in January, his native Poland in June, and Ireland and the United States in early fall. The pope repeatedly demonstrated a strict commitment to traditional Catholic doctrine and discipline. He reaffirmed the requirement for priestly celibacy and made clear his opposition to the ordination of women. He also called for a return to traditional garb for nuns.

His journey to Poland marked the first time a pope had ever entered a communist country. It was estimated that some six million people saw and heard the pope during the visit. In the fall, he also became the first pope to tour Ireland, a staunchly Catholic country. From there, he proceeded to the United States, where he addressed the United Nations General Assembly and conferred with President Carter. His tour also took him to Boston, Philadelphia, Des Moines, and Chicago; enthusiastic crowds greeted him at each stop.

DRAPER HILL
Courtesy Detroit News

KEN ALEXANDER
Courtesy San Francisco Examiner

JEFF MACNELLY
Richmond News Leader
©Chicago Tribune—New York
News Syndicate

SHOES OF THE FISHERMAN

JIM DOBBINS
*Courtesy Manchester
Union-Leader*

CHESTER COMMODORE
Courtesy Chicago Daily Defender

ROB LAWLOR
Courtesy Philadelphia Daily News

The IRA

One of Great Britain's most revered World War II heroes, Lord Earl Mountbatten, was assassinated in August while on vacation in northwest Ireland—the victim of a bomb planted by members of the Provisional Irish Republican Army.

Political terrorism increased in Ireland during the year, and across-the-border attacks by the IRA could no longer by concealed. To stress its abhorrence of IRA terrorism, the British government offered a reward totaling more than $200,000 for information leading to the apprehension of Mountbatten's murderers.

Two men were arrested and charged with the crime. After a fourteen-day trial, one was convicted and sent to prison for life. The other was acquitted.

BOB ALEXANDER
*Courtesy Eagle-Tribune,
Lawrence, Mass.*

DRAPER HILL
Courtesy Detroit News

Shamrock of Thorns

EDDIE GERMANO
Courtesy Brockton Daily Enterprise

" SOMEDAY, SON, ALL THIS CAN BE YOURS. "

M. G. LORD
Courtesy Newsday

Three Mile Island

One of the most highly publicized events of the year was the nuclear plant breakdown at Three Mile Island near Middletown, Pennsylvania.

First reports of the incident suggested only a minor accident at the plant's Unit 2 reactor. This, however, quickly became front-page news and a wave of near-panic swept over the area. Anti-nuclear demonstrations were staged in many U.S. cities, as well as abroad.

A dangerous meltdown was considered a distinct possibility since portions of the reactor core were exposed. In addition, tiny amounts of low-level radiation had seeped into the atmosphere. Thousands of residents fled the area around the plant after Pennsylvania Governor Richard Thornburgh recommended that small children and pregnant women be evacuated as a precautionary measure.

Thirteen days later, the governor announced that it was safe to return to the area. Several investigations were initiated, including one by a special presidential commission. The commission report criticized the expertise of plant employees and recommended better plans to deal with future emergencies of that nature.

BOB ENGLEHART
Courtesy Dayton Journal Herald

S. C. RAWLS
Courtesy Palm Beach Post

Great "IT'LL NEVER HAPPEN" moments in history....

THE SINKING OF THE TITANIC...

THE HINDENBURG DISASTER...

THE FIRST FLIGHT...

THE '69 METS...

A MAN ON THE MOON...

A NUCLEAR POWER ACCIDENT...

PAUL SZEP
Courtesy Boston Globe

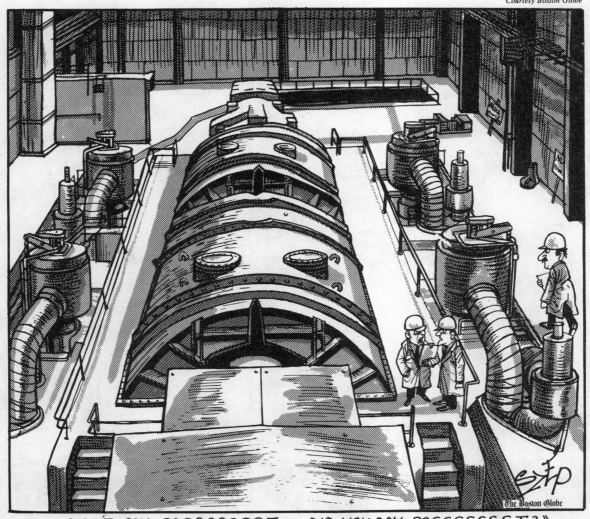

"I DIDN'T SAY PSSSSSSSST... DID YOU SAY PSSSSSSSST?"

MERLE TINGLEY
Courtesy London (Can.) Free Press

JOHN COLLINS
Courtesy Montreal (Can.) Gazette

DR. JEKYLL and MR. HIDE

ROGER HARVELL
*Courtesy Pine Bluff (Ark.)
Commercial*

OOPS!

HY ROSEN
Courtesy Albany Times-Union

"YOU GOTTA ADMIT — IT'S A HELLUVA' ENVIRONMENT!"

129

CHUCK AYERS
Courtesy Akron Beacon Journal

"Isn't this darling! Oil from the Mexican oil spill! Let's get one to go with our Three Mile Island souvenir."

JIM BERRY
©NEA

The Human Factor

TOM FLANNERY
Courtesy Baltimore Sun

"Probably a bunch of them anti-nuclear weirdos!"

BILL GRAHAM
Courtesy Arkansas Gazette

ROB LAWLOR
Courtesy Philadelphia Daily News

The DC-10

A DC-10 crashed on takeoff at Chicago's O'Hare International Airport on May 25 after its left engine was ripped away. The crash, which occurred less than a mile from the airport, killed 273 persons and launched a major inquiry into the safety of the DC-10 design. All 138 of the DC-10s operating in America were immediately grounded for inspection of the pylons that attach the engines to the wings.

After a seven-month investigation, the National Transportation Safety Board announced that the carrier involved, American Airlines, must shoulder the major responsibility for the crash because of inadequate maintenance procedures. The board also determined that the Federal Aviation Administration and McDonnell Douglas Corporation, builder of the DC-10, shared the blame.

DAVE GRANLUND
Courtesy Middlesex News

TIM MENEES
*Courtesy Pittsburgh
Post-Gazette*

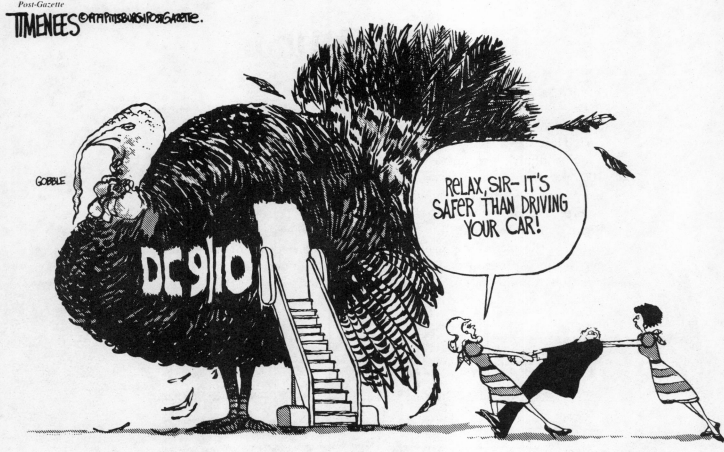

ROBERT GRAYSMITH
Courtesy San Francisco Chronicle

The new improved DC-10

CHUCK AYERS
*Courtesy Akron Beacon
Journal*

The Killer Rabbit

A rabbit and President Carter combined to make headlines in August. While fishing in a lake near his hometown of Plains, Georgia, Carter was attacked by what the press termed a "killer rabbit."

According to the president, he actually had to fight off the cottontail with a paddle to prevent it from climbing aboard his boat.

BRIAN BASSET
Courtesy Seattle Times

133

NOTHIN' TO WORRY ABOUT

JIM LANGE
The Daily Oklahoman
©The Oklahoma Publishing Co.

"MY NAME'S HARVEY — AND WHAT'S THIS STORY I KEEP HEARING?"

CHARLES BROOKS
Courtesy Birmingham (Ala.) News

RAY OSRIN
Courtesy Cleveland Plain Dealer

134

KEN ALEXANDER
Courtesy San Francisco Examiner

RUFUS PAPENFUS
Courtesy Fresno Guide

THE CUBAN CRISIS

ANOTHER RABBIT!

THAT'S THE THING ABOUT RABBITS· THEY MULTIPLY.

CHARLES WERNER
Courtesy Indianapolis Star

AND YOU SHOULD HAVE SEEN HIS FACE WHEN I HISSED HIM

HE'S NOT TOO POPULAR WITH FROGS EITHER

SUNDAY NEWS-JOURNAL 9-©1979

JACK JURDEN
Courtesy Wilmington News-Journal

RUFUS PAPENFUS
Courtesy Fresno Guide

"LADEEEES AND GENTLEMENNN... THE PRES'DENT OF THE W...NITED STATES!...".

Latin America

Anastasio Somoza Debayle, Nicaragua's military strongman, was overthrown by guerillas in 1979, ending his family's forty-six-year reign in that Latin American nation. After ten months of fighting without aid from the U.S., Somoza fled the country, which is now ruled by the Sandinista National Liberation Front.

President Carter paid a visit to Mexico's President Lopez Portillo and received a public scolding from his host for America's past treatment of Mexico. The problem of illegal Mexican immigration to the U.S. went unsolved, and Carter returned without a promise of increased shipments of Mexican oil to America.

Cuban President Fidel Castro visited the U.S. in October and addressed the United Nations General Assembly in his role as chairman of the so-called non-aligned countries. He devoted most of his speech to denouncing the United States and called upon wealthy nations to create a $300 billion fund to aid developing nations.

ED VALTMAN
©Rothco

'YOU ONLY HAVE TO ASSURE ME YOU HAVE NO EVIL INTENTIONS AND I WON'T MIND YOUR STAYING'

ELDON PLETCHER
New Orleans Times-Picayune
©Rothco

¡Gas, plis!

LUIS BORJA
Courtesy Caricatura Nacional

JON KENNEDY
Courtesy Arkansas Democrat

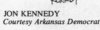
Ten feet tall

BOB SULLIVAN
Courtesy Worcester Telegram

ROY PETERSON
Courtesy Vancouver Sun

LEW HARSH
Courtesy Scranton Times

". . .and Cuba wishes to express its appreciation to Vietnam for its solidarity and support of our stand at this summit of non-aligned nations. . ."

BILL DE ORE
Courtesy Dallas Morning News

THE LAST DAYS OF SOMOZA

Caricatura Nacional

Por BORJA

Barrera Fronteriza

TODAY SPEARS, TOMORROW CANNON

LUIS BORJA
Courtesy Caricatura Nacional

JOHN TREVER
Courtesy Albuquerque
Journal

W. SOLO
Courtesy Instituto
Costarricense de
Electricidad, Costa Rica

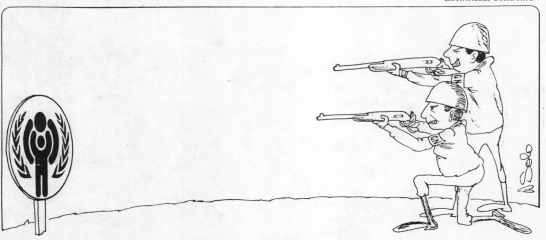

INTERNATIONAL YEAR OF THE CHILD

Canadian Politics

A virtual unknown, Joe Clark, became the youngest prime minister in Canada's history when May elections ousted eleven-year veteran Pierre Elliott Trudeau.

The country's balance of trade showed a surplus for the first six months of the year of $990 million, roughly half of the surplus for the same period in the previous year. Imports climbed by 28 percent, with the major rise occurring in steel and heavy machinery. Textiles, especially synthetic fiber yarns and mixed fiber fabrics, increased by one third.

The 1979 meeting of the General Agreement on Tariffs and Trade endorsed accords to cut tariffs and to lower many other trade barriers in farm and industrial products. GATT failed, however, to agree on new regulations to restrict disruptive imports.

Quebec's Premier Rene Levesque announced that he will seek a mandate from Quebec voters to negotiate the French-speaking province's secession from Canada "based on the equality of nations."

ROY CARLESS
Courtesy Canadian Transport

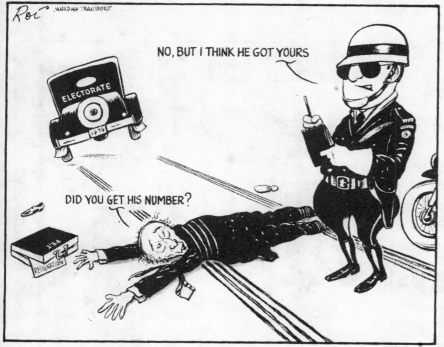

JOHN COLLINS
Courtesy Montreal (Can.) Gazette

GETTING READY FOR THE DUEL

"LOOK AL, I'M MAD AT QUEBEC TOO...BUT MOVING OUR HEAD OFFICE?"

NEW TENANTS AT 24 SUSSEX DRIVE

'For a while there we thought they had us over a barrel'

In Memoriam

Among the notables who died during 1979 were the following:

Edgar Buchanan, actor; Al Capp, comic strip cartoonist who created Li'l Abner and the world of Dogpatch; Philippe Cousteau, son of Jacques Cousteau; John George Diefenbaker, former prime minister of Canada; Mamie Eisenhower, wife of Dwight D. Eisenhower; Arthur Fiedler, conductor of the Boston Pops; Tony Galento, former heavyweight boxer; Warren Giles, former president of the National Baseball League; Conrad Hilton, financier; Barbara Hutton, Woolworth heiress; Emmett Kelly, circus clown; Lord Mountbatten, British war hero; Thurman Munson, catcher for the New York Yankees; Nelson Rockefeller, former vice-president; and John Wayne, actor.

DICK WALLMEYER
Long Beach Press-Telegram
©Register and Tribune Syndicate

CHARLES BROOKS
Courtesy Birmingham (Ala.) News

CLYDE WELLS
Courtesy Augusta (Ga.) Chronicle

...S'LONG, DUKE...BE SEEIN'Y'...

JOHN WAYNE 1907-1979

VERN THOMPSON
Courtesy Lawton (Okla.) Constitution

JOHN 'DUKE' WAYNE 1907-1979

BERT WHITMAN
Courtesy Phoenix Gazette

DICK WALLMEYER
Long Beach Press-Telegram
©Register and Tribune Syndicate

ROBERT GRAYSMITH
Courtesy San Francisco Chronicle

"Awright, Pilgrims, let's get those clouds in a circle"

147

UNFORGETTABLE

BLAINE
Courtesy The Spectator, Canada

"...TAKE THIS SEAT, MAESTRO!"

Baldy

BALDY
Courtesy Atlanta Constitution

148

. . . And Other Issues

Margaret Thatcher became the first woman prime minister in Great Britain's history when she assumed that office on May 4. In the U.S., the city of Chicago also elected its first woman mayor, Jane Byrne.

American farmers staged new demonstrations in the nation's capital in 1979, parading their tractors through the city and calling for parity prices for their products.

A coroner's jury was convened at Matthews Ridge, Guyana, early in 1979 to probe one of history's most horrible events—the mass deaths and/or suicides of more than nine hundred cultists at the People's Temple commune in Jonestown, Guyana. The jury determined that the Rev. Jim Jones had used his psychological power over cult members to induce them to take their own lives.

"Ahoy! Margaret Thatcher here! I'm your new pilot!"

HUGH HAYNIE
© 1979 The Courier-Journal
HUGH HAYNIE
Louisville Courier-Journal
©Los Angeles Times Syndicate

DANA SUMMERS
*Courtesy Fayetteville
(N. C.) Times*

"IF IT WORKS ON ARTHRITIS, IT MUST WORK ON HEADACHES"

'Big deal, Henry . . . we've seen it all before.'

PAUL SZEP
Courtesy Boston Globe

JERRY ROBINSON
©Cartoonists and Writers
Snydicate

LEONARD NORRIS
Courtesy Vancouver (Can.) Sun

"Save wildlife, save parkland, save whales, save energy . . . never any mention of string or tin foil

CHARLES DANIEL
Courtesy Knoxville Journal

ED STEIN
*Courtesy Rocky Mountain
News*

JOHN BRANCH
Courtesy Chapel Hill News

GOVERNMENT
OF THE PEOPLE
BY THE PEOPLE
AND
FOR THE PEOPLE

'Now Here's The Cornerstone We Want To Replace'

COMING INTO FOCUS

BEER FOUND TO CONTAIN CANCER-CAUSING AGENTS — NEWS ITEM.

NIGHT FLIGHT FROM GUYANA

"SAY AH!"

BOB BECKETT
*Courtesy Burlington County
(N. J.) Times*

WAYNE STAYSKAL
Courtesy Chicago Tribune

"WOULD YOU LIKE A SINGLE ROOM FOR $362.00 A DAY, A DOUBLE ROOM FOR $235.00, OR FILE DRAWER B FOR $117.00?"

In For Repairs

REG MANNING
Courtesy Arizona Republic

DRAPER HILL
Courtesy Detroit News

Past Award Winners

PULITZER PRIZE EDITORIAL CARTOON

1922—Rollin Kirby, New York World
1924—J. N. Darling, New York Herald Tribune
1925—Rollin Kirby, New York World
1926—D. R. Fitzpatrick, St. Louis Post-Dispatch
1927—Nelson Harding, Brooklyn Eagle
1928—Nelson Harding, Brooklyn Eagle
1929—Rollin Kirby, New York World
1930—Charles Macauley, Brooklyn Eagle
1931—Edmund Duffy, Baltimore Sun
1932—John T. McCutcheon, Chicago Tribune
1933—H. M. Talburt, Washington Daily News
1934—Edmund Duffy, Baltimore Sun
1935—Ross A. Lewis, Milwaukee Journal
1937—C. D. Batchelor, New York Daily News
1938—Vaughn Shoemaker, Chicago Daily News
1939—Charles G. Werner, Daily Oklahoman
1940—Edmund Duffy, Baltimore Sun
1941—Jacob Burck, Chicago Times
1942—Herbert L. Block, Newspaper Enterprise Association
1943—Jay N. Darling, New York Herald Tribune
1944—Clifford K. Berryman, Washington Star
1945—Bill Mauldin, United Feature Syndicate
1946—Bruce Russell, Los Angeles Times
1947—Vaughn Shoemaker, Chicago Daily News
1948—Reuben L. (Rube) Goldberg, New York Sun
1949—Lute Pease, Newark Evening News
1950—James T. Berryman, Washington Star
1951—Reginald W. Manning, Arizona Republic
1952—Fred L. Packer, New York Mirror
1953—Edward D. Kuekes, Cleveland Plain Dealer
1954—Herbert L. Block, Washington Post
1955—Daniel R. Fitzpatrick, St. Louis Post-Dispatch
1956—Robert York, Louisville Times
1957—Tom Little, Nashville Tennessean
1958—Bruce M. Shanks, Buffalo Evening News
1959—Bill Mauldin, St. Louis Post-Dispatch
1961—Carey Orr, Chicago Tribune
1962—Edmund S. Valtman, Hartford Times
1963—Frank Miller, Des Moines Register
1964—Paul Conrad, Denver Post
1966—Don Wright, Miami News
1967—Patrick B. Oliphant, Denver Post
1968—Eugene Gray Payne, Charlotte Observer
1969—John Fischetti, Chicago Daily News
1970—Thomas F. Darcy, Newsday
1971—Paul Conrad, Los Angeles Times
1972—Jeffrey K. MacNelly, Richmond News Leader
1974—Paul Szep, Boston Globe
1975—Garry Trudeau, Universal Press Syndicate
1976—Tony Auth, Philadelphia Enquirer
1977—Paul Szep, Boston Globe
1978—Jeff MacNelly, Richmond News Leader
1979—Bob Englehart, Dayton Journal Herald*

* Selected by Pulitzer editorial committee

NOTE: Pulitzer Prize Award was not given 1923, 1936, 1960, 1965, and 1973.

SIGMA DELTA CHI AWARD EDITORIAL CARTOON

1942—Jacob Burck, Chicago Times
1943—Charles Werner, Chicago Sun
1944—Henry Barrow, Associated Press
1945—Reuben L. Goldberg, New York Sun
1946—Dorman H. Smith, Newspaper Enterprise Association
1947—Bruce Russell, Los Angeles Times
1948—Herbert Block, Washington Post
1949—Herbert Block, Washington Post
1950—Bruce Russell, Los Angeles Times
1951—Herbert Block, Washington Post, and
        Bruce Russell, Los Angeles Times
1952—Cecil Jensen, Chicago Daily News
1953—John Fischetti, Newspaper Enterprise Association
1954—Calvin Alley, Memphis Commercial Appeal
1955—John Fischetti, Newspaper Enterprise Association
1956—Herbert Block, Washington Post
1957—Scott Long, Minneapolis Tribune
1958—Clifford H. Baldowski, Atlanta Constitution
1959—Charles G. Brooks, Birmingham News
1960—Dan Dowling, New York Herald-Tribune
1961—Frank Interlandi, Des Moines Register
1962—Paul Conrad, Denver Post
1963—William Mauldin, Chicago Sun-Times
1964—Charles Bissell, Nashville Tennessean
1965—Roy Justus, Minneapolis Star
1966—Patrick Oliphant, Denver Post
1967—Eugene Payne, Charlotte Observer
1968—Paul Conrad, Los Angeles Times
1969—William Mauldin, Chicago Sun-Times
1970—Paul Conrad, Los Angeles Times
1971—Hugh Haynie, Louisville Courier-Journal
1972—William Mauldin, Chicago Sun-Times
1973—Paul Szep, Boston Globe
1974—Mike Peters, Dayton Daily News

1975—Tony Auth, Philadelphia Enquirer
1976—Paul Szep, Boston Globe
1977—Don Wright, Miami News
1978—Jim Borgman, Cincinnati Enquirer

NATIONAL NEWSPAPER AWARD/CANADA EDITORIAL CARTOON

1949—Jack Boothe, Toronto Globe and Mail
1950—James G. Reidford, Montreal Star
1951—Len Norris, Vancouver Sun
1952—Robert La Palme, Le Devoir, Montreal
1953—Robert W. Chambers, Halifax Chronicle-Herald
1954—John Collins, Montreal Gazette
1955—Merle R. Tingley, London Free Press
1956—James G. Reidford, Toronto Globe and Mail
1957—James G. Reidford, Toronto Globe and Mail
1958—Raoul Hunter, Le Soleil, Quebec

1959—Duncan Macpherson, Toronto Star
1960—Duncan Macpherson, Toronto Star
1961—Ed McNally, Montreal Star
1962—Duncan Macpherson, Toronto Star
1963—Jan Kamienski, Winnipeg Tribune
1964—Ed McNally, Montreal Star
1965—Duncan Macpherson, Toronto Star
1966—Robert W. Chambers, Halifax Chronicle-Herald
1967—Raoul Hunter, Le Soleil, Quebec
1968—Roy Peterson, Vancouver Sun
1969—Edward Uluschak, Edmonton Journal
1970—Duncan Macpherson, Toronto Daily Star
1971—Yardley Jones, Toronto Sun
1972—Duncan Macpherson, Toronto Star
1973—John Collins, Montreal Gazette
1974—Blaine, Hamilton Spectator
1975—Roy Peterson, Vancouver Sun
1976—Andy Donato, Toronto Sun
1977—Terry Mosher, Montreal Gazette
1978—Terry Mosher, Montreal Gazette

Index

INDEX